ALL-STAR SPORTS PUZZLES

Basketball

GAMES, TRIVIA, QUIZZES AND MORE!

Jesse Ross

RAINCOAST BOOKS

www.raincoast.com

Dedicated to Luba.
Thank you for everything.

Raincoast Books gratefully acknowledges the financial support of the Province of British Columbia through the BC Arts Council and the Book Publishing Tax Credit and the Government of Canada through the Canada Council for the Arts, and the Book Publishing Industry Development Program (BPIDP).

Edited by Brian Scrivener
Cover design by Teresa Bubela
Interior design by Warren Clark

Library and Archives Canada Cataloguing in Publication

Ross, Jesse, 1986-
    All-star sports puzzles : basketball / Jesse Paul Ross.

    ISBN 13: 978-1-55192-822-7
    ISBN 10: 1-55192-822-1

    1. Puzzles—Juvenile literature. 2. Basketball—Miscellanea—Juvenile
literature. I. Title.   GV1493.R65 2007   j793.73   C2007-900491-1

Library of Congress Control Number: 2007921216

Raincoast Books   In the United States:
9050 Shaughnessy Street   Publishers Group West
Vancouver, British Columbia   1700 Fourth Street
Canada V6P 6E5   Berkeley, California
www.raincoast.com   94710

Raincoast Books is committed to protecting the environment and to the responsible use of natural resources. We are working with suppliers and printers to phase out our use of paper produced from ancient forests. This book is printed with vegetable-based inks on 100% ancient-forest-free, 40% post-consumer recycled, processed chlorine- and acid-free paper. For further information, visit our website at www.raincoast.com/publishing/

Printed in Canada by Webcom

10 9 8 7 6 5 4 3 2 1

CONTENTS

Trivia

Matching

Fill Me In

Puzzles

Long Puzzles

Note: Throughout the book, you will find additional facts at the bottom of each page, and occasionally a **Bonus question**. ??? These are extra hard questions for expert basketball fans only!

Check out our website at **www.allstarsportspuzzles.com**

Note: All puzzles are accurate, to the best of our knowledge, as of September, 2007.

Mixed Up Names

We've mixed up the first and last names of these star players.
See if you can find their proper match!

Amare	Douglas
Brad	Kirilenko
Marcus	Miller
Zydrunas	Leslie
Katie	Stoudemire
Tamika	Brand
Lisa	Anthony
Lauren	Marion
Sheryl	Arenas
Shawn	Garnett
Elton	Catchings
Andrei	Camby
Carmelo	Ilgauskas
Gilbert	Paul
Chris	Swoopes
Kevin	Jackson

Libyan Suleiman Ali Nashnush is reportedly the tallest player ever, measuring in at 8 feet 1/4 inches when he played for their national team.

The Great Search

The last names of 19 of the top scorers in NBA history are hidden below. They are written forwards or backwards, and hidden diagonally, horizontally and vertically. When you have found them all, the leftover letters spell out the name of the 20th all-time scorer.

E	N	G	L	I	S	H	C	L	M	M
R	I	N	A	D	R	O	J	A	A	I
M	A	L	O	N	E	L	W	E	L	L
R	L	B	I	R	D	Y	E	N	O	L
O	R	O	B	E	R	T	S	O	N	E
L	E	D	E	A	T	E	T	H	E	R
Y	B	O	L	A	J	U	W	O	N	E
A	M	E	G	L	I	L	D	I	E	E
B	A	R	K	L	E	Y	U	D	N	R
R	H	Y	E	L	T	N	A	D	E	G
X	C	W	I	L	K	I	N	S	B	L
E	K	E	C	I	L	V	A	H	R	A

Names

Kareem ABDUL-JABBAR	Patrick EWING	Hakeem OLAJUWON
Charles BARKLEY	Hal GREER	Shaquille O'NEAL
Elgin BAYLOR	John HAVLICEK	Oscar ROBERTSON
Larry BIRD	Michael JORDAN	Jerry WEST
Wilt CHAMBERLAIN	Karl MALONE	Dominique WILKINS
Adrian DANTLEY	Moses MALONE	
Alex ENGLISH	Reggie MILLER	

Ted St. Martin holds the Guinness World Record for most consecutive free-throws made, with 5,221.

20th All-Time Scorer:

_ _ _ _ _ " _ _ _ _ _ _

In the Lane

Each of these random rows of letters has a basketball-related word, name or team hidden within. You must fill in the one missing letter in the centre to reveal the word. For example, with "A F R E N C L I ___ P E R S I N D S", add a P to the centre to reveal the word "Clippers".

S E T R O S Y A	_____	M I N G E S A M
H A M E A R D U	_____	K E T E A M O N
L O S T E A M A	_____	O R D A N T I S
C R I E S T R A	_____	E L L I N G O S
Q U I L E T I N	_____	A F I N A L S O
S T R I P L E D	_____	U B L E S T E V
S C O R P E R S	_____	N A L F O U L D
D R E A R E B A	_____	K E T I N D E R
H E A L T E R E	_____	E L T I C S T O
R E S H E R A P	_____	O R S I T E D A
M I N D S H O R	_____	A V A L I E R S
S C A R E B O U	_____	D E L T I N G T

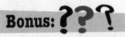
Bonus:

Can you name the five most recent teams to join the NBA, not including teams that moved from other cities?

True or False

Can you figure out which of these is true or false? Circle your choice.

1) Lakers' power forward Vladimir Radmanovic does more than play basketball. He has performed live on stage as The Grandfather in The Nutcracker ballet.

True   **False**

2) In 2002, retired NBA player Matt Geiger made news because his 4,400-pound pet bison, "Big Daddy", jumped a fence at his home and escaped.

True   **False**

3) A 1998 game between Cleveland and Milwaukee was cancelled because people kept disrupting the game. Five separate times, groups of individuals walked onto the court, protesting Nike's connection with sweatshops.

True   **False**

4) In 2006, NBA teams played pre-season games in Lyon (France), Cologne (Germany), Moscow (Russia) and Monterrey (Mexico).

True   **False**

5) Kobe Bryant's amazing 81-point game on January 22, 2006, was his 666th career game.

True   **False**

6) NBA players are huge celebrities in Asia. The Official Ben Wallace Fan Club has 34,505 members, and their website claims 29,550 of those are from Asia.

True   **False**

7) A 2005 game between Orlando and Detroit was delayed because a seeing-eye dog relieved itself under Detroit's basket. The dog was part of a charity ceremony.

True   **False**

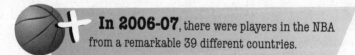

In 2006-07, there were players in the NBA from a remarkable 39 different countries.

8) Yao Ming is married and has nine children.

True   **False**

9) Mark Cuban, the Dallas Mavericks' eccentric owner, was banned from attending games in Sacramento. Why? Because in a 2004 pre-season game he ran onto the court and grabbed the ball away from one of the Kings' players.

True   **False**

10) On September 21, 2006, the Russian national team defeated the USA in the semi-finals of FIBA's women's basketball championship. This was the USA's first international loss since 1994, ending a 51-game winning streak.

True   **False**

11) The man who invented basketball, James Naismith, played only two games in his life.

True   **False**

12) The Boston Celtics 18-game losing streak in 2007 was the longest in franchise history, "beating" the previous record of 13. By comparison, the Mavericks (formed 34 years after the Celtics) have already had eight 15-game losing streaks.

True   **False**

13) Michael Jordan has officially retired from playing basketball a record five times (in 1985, 1993, 1999, 2002 and 2003).

True   **False**

14) Loyola Marymount has played in 11 of the 16 all-time highest-scoring Division I men's games, winning eight times. The highest-scoring game had a combined total of 331 points.

True   **False**

15) The 2005 San Antonio Spurs were NBA Champions. The strange thing was they only used nine different players throughout the whole year.

True   **False**

There are approximately 4,000,000 kids playing basketball at a pre-high school level in the USA, but only 442 players in the NBA.

Dream Teams

Three of these 12 defunct NBA franchises are made up. Can you spot the fakes?

Anderson Packers	Baltimore Bullets
Chicago Stags	Connecticut Ballers
Indianapolis Olympians	Newark Statesmen
Pittsburgh Ironmen	Providence Steamrollers
Sheboygan Redskins	Trenton Marauders
Toronto Huskies	Waterloo Hawks

The NBA's shortest player award goes to Muggsy Bogues, who stood 5 feet 3 inches. Notable mention goes to Anthony "Spud" Webb, 5 feet 7 inches, who won the dunk competition in 1986.

Hidden Teams

Six NBA team names are hidden below, starting with the central letter C and extending out. The letters can be connected on either side, above, below or diagonally. The same letter cannot be used twice in the same name. We've used either the city or franchise name of the team (i.e., Washington or Wizards). Watch out, one name is hidden twice!

T	A	R	S	P	V	T	A	O
E	P	E	V	E	E	L	C	G
P	I	I	L	L	H	I	A	N
L	E	V	A	C	E	A	R	D
R	A	I	H	A	H	L	N	E
G	S	C	T	V	L	A	T	D
O	A	E	T	O	R	I	C	S

Bonus: ???

The days of American dominance at the Olympics are coming to an end, with many countries now competing at an exceptionally high level. Can you name the medalists from 2004 in Athens, in both the men's and women's tournaments? What about 2000 in Sydney?

Round and Round

Fill the answers to the clues into the grid below, beginning with #1 in the upper left corner, and working clockwise around the grid. The last one or two letters from each answer form the beginning of the next answer. If you can't get one clue, try moving on to the next and working backwards. The number in parentheses beside each clue indicates the number of letters in the answer.

1) Hometown of the most recent team to join the NBA, in 2004 (9)

2) "There's no 'I' in _____" (4)

3) 48 of these in a game (7)

4) A great defensive play (5)

5) This Game occurs once per season (7)

6) Often follows a missed shot (7)

7) Runner-up in 05-06 (6)

8) Hook - _____ (4)

9) Causes overtime (3)

10) One of the conferences (7)

11) Vince Carter moved to this franchise in 2005 (4)

12) Golden _____ (5)

13) Big _____ (3)

14) Formerly the BAA (3)

15) Player who doesn't pass (7)

16) Games played, abbreviation (2)

Anat Draigor, considered Israel's best women's basketball player, recently returned from a 10-year retirement. On her 46th birthday, Anat scored an amazing 136 points in a league game.

							2
1							
				7			
	11			12			
6							3
				16	13	8	
			15	14			
			10		9		
		5			4		

Bonus: ???

Four players in NBA history have recorded a quadruple-double. David Robinson was the last to do it, in 1994 (34 points, 10 blocks, 10 rebounds, 10 assists). Can you name the other three?

Lost Letters

Fill in the missing letter in the middle to complete the last letter of the player's name on the left, and the first letter of the player on the right. The missing letters, taken from top to bottom, spell out the name of the MVP in the first-ever NBA All-Star Game.

Dwyane Wad	_____	arl Watson
Jason Kid	_____	amon Stoudamire
Joey Graha	_____	alik Rose
Charlie Villanuev	_____	mir Johnson
Nenad Krsti	_____	hauncey Billups
Andre Iguodal	_____	lan Anderson
Dan Dicka	_____	ros Slokar
Charlie Bel	_____	uther Head
Ronald Dupre	_____	meka Okafor
Tracy McGrad	_____	ao Ming

* MVP of first All-Star game:

_____

Bonus: ???

Most people know how dominant the Boston Celtics have been in NBA history, with 16 Championship titles. Can you name the next six franchises with the most titles?

Your Choice

See if you can pick the right answer.

1) Hall-of-Famer Calvin Murphy was a great basketball player, but he was also a national champion in another sport. What sport was it?

A) Juggling
B) Baton Twirling
C) Tennis
D) Ping-Pong

2) Rick Barry led the league in free-throw shooting six times, and finished with a career average of 90% from the line. What was so strange about his free-throws?

A) He shot the ball underhanded.
B) He had a prosthetic arm, forcing him to shoot using only one hand.
C) Barry made nearly all his free-throws by banking the ball off the backboard.
D) In his first two seasons in the league, Berry had abysmal free-throw averages of 27% and 28%.

3) Which of the following was never a rule in basketball?

A) The player dribbling the ball was not allowed to shoot.
B) There was a jump ball at centre after every basket was scored.
C) The baskets used to be closed at the bottom, so the ball had to be retrieved after every point with a ladder.
D) Players had to play shirtless (to stop defenders from holding onto jerseys).

4) Which one of these strange stories is NOT true?

A) Dirk Nowitzki strained a tendon in his foot while trying to put on his shoe.
B) Drew Gooden of Orlando had infected hair follicles in his right leg.
C) Muggsy Bogues came down with chicken pox in 1999.
D) Paul Pierce missed three games after straining a back muscle during an elaborate dunk celebration.

5) What are the two most common jersey numbers of active players in the NBA (both worn by 20 players in 2006-07)?

A) 10 and 20
B) 19 and 9
C) 1 and 3
D) 7 and 8

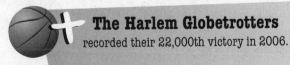

The Harlem Globetrotters recorded their 22,000th victory in 2006.

6) Rasheed Wallace had his NBA Championship ring altered. Why?

A) So it would fit on his middle finger.

B) To add the insignia "MLN", standing for Mia, Lana and Nashawn — the names of his children.

C) He had the ring altered into a gold tooth, which now covers his upper left bicuspid.

D) All of the above. (Wallace has won three rings in his career, and has altered each one.)

7) What is "SlamBall"?

A) A term commentator Marv Albert coined to describe the state of NBA basketball in the late 1990s, referring to the excessive physical contact.

B) A sport that involves two teams, a basketball and a bunch of trampolines built into the court. Yes, it's crazy.

C) Released in 1992 for the Sega Genesis, SlamBall has gone on to become the best-selling B-ball video game ever.

D) A specially designed Wilson ball that bounces twice as high as the regular ball.

8) Which one of the following has Dennis Rodman NOT done?

A) Skipped practice with the Bulls to wrestle alongside Hulk Hogan in the WCW. (They lost to Lex Luger and The Giant.)

B) Kicked an on-court photographer in the groin.

C) Got a tattoo on his back with the words "The Best Ever".

D) Led the league in rebounds per game seven years in a row, from 1992 through 1998.

9) What strange thing happened on opening night in San Antonio on November 11, 1994?

A) Due to a malfunction in the building, a large water cannon started spraying the crowd with water after the opening ceremony fireworks.

B) The visiting Trail Blazers had been hit by a flu bug, and started the game with only four players. The game was cancelled at half-time, with the Spurs leading 49-10.

C) Through a promotional contest with the NBA, a fan (Mark Mathelson) won a minute of playing time with the Spurs. He missed one jump shot and fouled Rod Strickland.

D) Midway through the third quarter, the power in the building went out. Luckily no one was hurt, but the game had to be re-scheduled.

Bailey Howell holds the NBA record for most personal fouls in one season. In 1964-65, Howell committed 345 personals, an average of 4.3 fouls per game.

Scrambled Terms

Can you unscramble these common basketball terms and expressions?

1) Cabbdoark _____

2) Erswent Ceefnorcen _____ _____

3) Valeglnirt _____

4) Zuzreb Trebea _____ _____

5) Failn Rouf _____ _____

6) Afts Kareb _____ _____

7) Eveesfind Brouned _____ _____

8) Werpo Dorrfaw _____ _____

9) Crahm Sneamds _____ _____

10) Eref Worth _____ _____

11) Chinacelt Olfu _____ _____

12) Dalgintenog _____

13) Pincpomahhis _____

Bonus: ???

Can you name the top five all-time NBA leaders in total blocks?

The Tip-Off

The player names below are listed according to their length. Fit them into their proper place in the grid; there is only one correct place for each word. To start you off, we filled in the name "May"; now look for a nine-letter word with Y as the fourth letter. Good luck!

3 Letters
Ebi
Ely
Lue
~~May~~

4 Letters
Ager
Bell
Ivey
Noel
Okur
Ross

5 Letters
Allen
Ellis
Elson
Green
Jones
Mason
O'Neal
Rondo
Smith
Swift
Udrih

6 Letters
Alston
Arenas
Benson
Greene
Hudson
Martin
Murphy
Najera
Norman

7 Letters
Delfind
Iverson
Pelacio
Roberts
Sampson
Simmons

8 Letters
Jeffries
Mourning
Peterson
Randolph

9 Letters
Armstrong
Przybilla
Stevenson

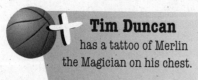

Tim Duncan has a tattoo of Merlin the Magician on his chest.

Joseph Odhiambo holds the Guinness World Record for spinning a basketball on one finger. How long did he last? 4 hours and 15 minutes. He also holds the record for continuously dribbling a basketball, at 26.5 hours straight.

20202400

What Am I?

See if you can figure out what these clues point towards, in as few clues as possible.

A

1) I'm an essential part of the game.

2) On rare occasions I've been known to fall down.

3) I'm not red, and I have nothing to do with a swish.

4) Players often kiss off me.

What am I? _____

B

1) I used to be part of a different sport, before I was changed.

2) In 2006 I was (briefly) changed again, for the first time in 35 years.

3) When I miss everything, people call it an "air me."

4) Hold on to me too long and you're travelling.

What am I? _____

In the U.S., basketball causes more injuries among people aged 15-24 than any other sport.

Know Your Teams

Can you figure out which NBA teams these clues point towards?

1) This team is all about numbers.

_____

2) Matadors tame this team.

_____

3) David Blaine and Penn & Teller know all about this team.

_____

4) Our solar system rotates around one of this team.

_____

5) This team is purely musical.

_____

6) This team is now extinct.

_____

7) This team swoops down from above to grab its prey.

_____

8) This team casts spells and uses the answer from question #3.

_____

9) This team can be sent to the moon, and even farther.

_____

Bonus: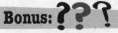

Four teams joined the NBA when it merged with the ABA in 1976. Can you name all four?

Skip to My Who?

See if you can match up these nicknames.

Magic	Michael Jordan
Air	Julius Erving
The Answer	Yao Ming
The Franchise	Wilt Chamberlain
Disco	Karl Malone
The Brazilian Blur	Leandro Barbosa
Dr. J	Hakeem Olajuwon
The Mailman	Allen Iverson
The Great Wall of China	Dennis Rodman
Skip To My Lou	Earvin Johnson
The Big Dipper	Steve Nash
The Worm	Steve Francis
The Dream	Dirk Nowitzki
Kid Canada	Dwyane Wade
Flash	Rafer Alston

The Boston Celtics won an amazing eight straight NBA Championships from 1959 to 1966, the longest streak of Championships in any major North American sport.

A Little History

Circle which year these clues point towards.

- The USA won gold in both the men's and women's tournament at the Olympics.
- The Houston Comets won their fourth-straight WNBA title, while the L.A. Lakers won their first NBA title since 1988. In college ball, Michigan State won the men's NCAA Division I tournament.
- For only the third time in history, two rookies (Elton Brand and Steve Francis) tied for Rookie of the Year.

1996   2000   2002

- Tim Duncan won both the regular season and playoff MVP awards, leading the Spurs to the title. The Detroit Shock became only the third franchise to win a WNBA title, defeating Los Angeles 2-1.
- LeBron James, Darko Milicic and Carmelo Anthony were drafted first, second and third overall. In the WNBA, LaToya Thomas, Chantelle Anderson and Cheryl Ford took the top three spots.
- For the first time ever, all NBA playoff series were played in a best-of-seven format.

2002   2003   2005

- The NBA's historic 50th season ends, marked by the return of teams to Canada, with the Toronto Raptors and the ill-fated Vancouver Grizzlies making their debut.
- The Chicago Bulls, with an astounding 87% winning average (including the regular season and playoffs) won the NBA title.
- In one of the best draft years in NBA history (10 of the 29 first-round picks have played in the All-Star Game), Kobe Bryant was not drafted until the 13th pick, while Steve Nash went 15th overall.

1993   1994   1996

Steve Hamilton is the only person to play in both the NBA Finals and baseball's World Series. Unfortunately, he did not win either title.

Word Work – Portland

See how many words you can make using only the letters in "Portland". They must be three letters or longer. We spotted 60; how many can you find? Here's the key:

0-10 words: Grade school star   30-40 words: Division I All-Star

10-20 words: High school star   40-50 words: NBA All-Star

20-30 words: Division II starter   50-60: Hall of Famer

P O R T L A N D

_____   _____   _____

_____   _____   _____

_____   _____   _____

_____   _____   _____

_____   _____   _____

_____   _____   _____

_____   _____   _____

_____   _____   _____

_____   _____   _____

_____   _____   _____

_____   _____   _____

_____   _____   _____

_____   _____   _____

_____   _____   _____

Bonus: ???

How many of the last 10 first-overall NBA draft picks can you name, going back to 1997?

It's a Numbers Game

See if you can fill in the correct answer, choosing from the numbers in the box below. Cross out each one as you go. This is one of the hardest puzzles in the book, so good luck.

1) Average attendance at NBA games in 1946-47:

_____

2) Average attendance at NBA games in 2005-06:

_____

3) Number of languages the 2006 NBA Finals was broadcast in:

_____

4) Total payroll of the 2006-07 New York Knicks, highest in the league:

_____

5) Total payroll of the 2006-07 Charlotte Bobcats, lowest in the league:

_____

6) Record number of consecutive games the Denver Nuggets registered over 100 points:

_____

7) Fewest points ever scored by an NBA team in one game (Bulls, 1999):

_____

8) Number of non-American players on NBA rosters in 2006-07:

_____

9) Number of teams in the NBA:

_____

10) Number of teams in the WNBA:

_____

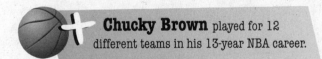

Chucky Brown played for 12 different teams in his 13-year NBA career.

11) Total number of minutes Kareem Abdul-Jabbar has played in the NBA, first all-time:

_____

12) Total career points for Kareem Abdul-Jabbar, first all-time:

_____

13) Average height of NBA players in 2006:

_____

14) Average weight of NBA players in 2006 (in pounds):

_____

15) Height of Raptors' centre Rafael Araujo:

_____

16) Height of Knicks' guard Nate Robinson, who beat Araujo to a jump ball in a 2006 game in Toronto:

_____

17) Career number of three-pointers Shaquille O'Neal has made, through 2006:

_____

18) Estimated number of people, worldwide, who watched Game 1 of the 2005 NBA Finals:

_____

1	46	136	17,558	41,333,581
14	49	221	38,378	105,000,000
30	82	3,142	57,446	139,381,526
	5'9"	6'11"	6'7"	

Highest scoring NBA game: 186–184, Detroit over Denver in 1983. Lowest scoring game: 19–18, Ft. Wayne over Minneapolis in 1950.

Pass the Buck

By changing only one letter at a time, can you make the top word become the bottom word? Be careful, each letter you substitute as you go must make a new word. For example, to change the word DARE into the word CORD, you could go: Dare - Care - Card - Cord.

1) Mavs

_____

_____

Nash

2) Man

_____

_____

Tie

3) Rose

_____

_____

_____

Pass

4) Pass

_____

_____

_____

Buck

5) Hook

_____

_____

Shot

6) Dunk

_____

_____

_____

Fold

The maximum WNBA team salary in 2007 is $700,000. By comparison, the minimum salary of a second-year NBA player in 2008 is $711,517.

Opening Night

Fill in the crossword grid by answering each clue, corresponding to the number in the grid.

Across

1) The leader of the team

3) NBA has a soft salary _____

5) Month commonly associated with madness

7) Necessary for an assist

8) Retired Knicks' great Patrick _____

9) Finger _____

12) Type of shot where the shooter moves backwards

13) Rejection

17) 2006 Champions

18) Young players hope to hear their name called at this event

19) Type of line, also known as base

Down

1) Chris Kaman and Alonzo Mourning's position

2) Too many steps

3) Training _____

4) Most common kind of foul

6) After a Championship in 1998, this team missed the playoffs six straight years

10) Type of Games

11) ____ Antonio

13) Common schoolyard game, uses two balls

14) Jason _____

15) Field _____

16) Follows a tie

Did you know: Bonzi Wells' real first name is Gawen, and Ray Allen's full name is Walter Ray Allen.

Hidden Teams #2

Six NBA team names are hidden below, starting with the central letter S and extending out. The letters can be connected on either side, above, below or diagonally. The same letter cannot be used twice in the same name. We've used either the city or franchise name of the team (i.e., Indiana or Pacers). Watch out, one name is hidden twice!

E	T	I	S	R	C	O	N	T
L	T	A	A	N	U	T	I	E
S	I	N	E	P	A	C	M	C
C	N	T	A	S	E	A	T	A
O	O	P	U	U	A	C	R	T
N	S	R	E	O	N	V	E	L
I	O	N	S	G	A	S	O	S

Bonus: ❓❓❓

Since expanding the field to 64 teams in 1985, what is the lowest-seeded team to win the NCAA Div. I tournament, through 2006? Extra credit for knowing the year.

Dream Arenas

Three of these 12 NBA arenas are made up. Can you spot the fakes?

Palace of Auburn Hills

Bradley Center

The Entertainment Palace

Rose Garden

The Pyramid

NEC/AMEX Center

Key Arena

Conseco Fieldhouse

Charlotte Bobcats Arena

The Rolling Stones Center

Quicken Loans Arena

Toyota Center

Bonus: ? ? ?

Can you name the top five all-time NBA leaders
in total assists?

Still in the Lane

Each of these random rows of letters has a basketball-related word, name or team hidden within. You must fill in the one missing letter in the centre to reveal the word.

1) HIZOEAGA ___ NETTSOMP

2) ESPERIME ___ ERASTHIN

3) CREASONI ___ RIBBLENT

4) PREASAWA ___ RIORSEAD

5) READREME ___ PHISEART

6) AGATRISC ___ UTCHISKA

7) TRECARME ___ OANTHONY

8) CRISPANC ___ ARTESEDS

9) SLEAMEMA ___ ERICKSED

10) ZACRATIN ___ TEALANTS

11) ARBENWAL ___ ACESTREM

12) JANECHAM ___ IONSHIPT

13) SHIREATE ___ MISTERRA

The 1972-73 76ers lost 73 games, almost equalling the number in their name. They won nine games all year.

Hard-Court Heroes

There have been some amazing accomplishments in the NBA, and some truly legendary individuals have made their mark. Below each name are four facts; three are true, and one is false. Can you spot the fake?

1) Wilt Chamberlain

A) In the 1961-62 season he averaged 50.4 points per game, and played 3,882 of a possible 3,890 minutes. (He was off the court for about eight seconds per game.)
B) In his 14-year NBA career, he never once fouled out of a game.
C) He once scored 100 points in an NBA game, when his Philadelphia Warriors beat the New York Knicks 169-147.
D) According to Wilt himself, he did not begin playing basketball until he turned 15.

2) Phil Jackson

A) He recorded 500 career coaching wins after only 682 total games, a 73% winning average.
B) No team coached by Jackson has lost more than 27 games in a regular season.
C) Three times, Jackson has coached a "three-peat", leading the Bulls to three consecutive Championships twice and the Lakers once. He is one of only three coaches to win Championships with different teams.
D) Jackson won a Championship as a player in 1973 with the Knicks.

3) Kobe Bryant

A) After being named the High School Player of the Year by multiple institutions, Kobe became the first guard drafted directly out of high school.
B) He had an astounding 81-point game in January 2006 against Toronto, the second-most points ever scored in a game. He shot 28-46 in just under 42 minutes of play. Earlier in the season, Kobe scored 62 points against Dallas. Amazingly, he only played three quarters that game.
C) Kobe is the youngest player to start an NBA game, start an All-Star Game, win the Dunk Competition, register 10,000 points and register 16,000 points.
D) He has won the league MVP twice, in 2001 and 2003. He also holds the record for most consecutive free-throws, with 101.

Wilt Chamberlain shot six of the top seven total free-throw attempts in a single season. However, he only holds one of the top 31 spots for total free-throws made in one season.

4) Lisa Leslie

A) Lisa was the first player to dunk in a WNBA game. She leads the WNBA with 5,412 career points, but also leads the league in turnovers.

B) In 2001, she was named MVP of the regular season, the All-Star Game and the WNBA Championship. She has gone on to win three regular season MVP awards and three Olympic gold medals.

C) She created a stir in late 2002 when she stated, during an interview with ESPN, that she was "better than 70% of the guys in the NBA." The interviewer responded, "I would say you're better than 95% of them!"

D) Lisa is also an aspiring model, having appeared in Vogue magazine, and has modelled clothes for Armani and Tommy Hilfiger.

5) Moses Malone

A) Malone, third on the all-time points list, is the only NBA player to play in four different decades, from 1969 through 1994.

B) He was the first player to lead the league in rebounds per game five years in a row. He is first all-time with 6,731 offensive rebounds, over 2,000 more than second place Robert Parish.

C) The first player to go directly from high school into the NBA, Moses was also remembered for some strange things, including the thick glasses he wore and his frequent number changes (he sported #2, #4, #6, #13, #22 and finally #24).

D) Moses did not foul out during the final 1,212 games of his career – the longest string of games without an ejection in history.

6) LeBron James

A) Before LeBron had even played a single NBA game, Nike had signed him to a $95 million contract to promote shoes.

B) In his 2006 playoff debut against Washington, LeBron became the first player to record a triple-double in four straight playoff games, leading the Cavs to victory four games to two. He finished the series with an amazing 30.8 points per game, 10.2 assists per game and 8.9 rebounds per game.

C) Only the second high school player ever drafted first-overall, LeBron went on to become the youngest player to ever record a triple-double and the youngest player to ever score 50 points in a game. He is also the youngest to ever win MVP at the All-Star Game or average 30 points per game over a season. Got all that?

D) Winning Rookie of the Year honours, he was one of only three players in history (alongside Michael Jordan and Oscar Robertson) to average over 20 points, five assists and five rebounds per game in their first year. At 19 years of age, he was the youngest Rookie of the Year winner.

Four girls have recorded at least 100 points in a high school game. Most notable was Lisa Leslie, who scored 101 points in one half. The opposing team forfeited, trailing 102-24.

Leading Ladies

The last names of the 19 all-time leading scorers in the WNBA are hidden below. They are written forwards or backwards, and hidden diagonally, horizontally and vertically. Watch out, a couple of names are hidden twice (Smith and Johnson). When you have found them all, the leftover letters spell out the last name of the 14th all-time scorer. Why her? Because her last name was too long for the puzzle!

M	E	T	H	O	M	P	S	O	N
G	R	I	F	F	I	T	H	C	D
R	E	M	L	A	P	W	I	Y	I
H	T	I	M	S	L	L	D	W	X
S	I	S	A	A	E	E	A	I	O
A	T	N	W	M	K	L	S	L	N
M	F	I	O	O	C	I	R	L	H
J	O	H	N	S	O	N	B	I	T
A	N	K	D	S	K	P	L	A	I
S	E	L	A	S	O	C	E	M	M
M	O	L	L	I	G	N	A	S	S
H	I	N	O	S	N	H	O	J	N

Names

Tamecka DIXON
Margo DYDEK
Jennifer GILLOM
Yolanda GRIFFITH
Chamique HOLDSCLAW
Lauren JACKSON
Shannon JOHNSON

Vickie JOHNSON
Lisa LESLIE
Mwadi MABIKA
Wendy PALMER
Nykesha SALES
Sheri SAM
Katie SMITH

Tangela SMITH
Andrea STINSON
Sheryl SWOOPES
Tina THOMPSON
Natalie WILLIAMS

The 1955 NBA Finals had to be moved from Ft. Wayne to Indianapolis. Why? There was a professional bowling tournament scheduled at the Ft. Wayne arena.

14th all-time WNBA scorer:

Taj _ - _ _ _ _ _ _ _

The Triple Dribble Puzzle

Fill in the word in the middle to complete both basketball expressions, terms or names. For example, by adding the word "Game" to "All-Star _____ Over", you get "All-Star Game" and "Game Over."

1) Orlando _____ Johnson

2) Jump _____ Clock

3) Triple _____ Dribble

4) Sixth _____ -to-Man

5) Turn _____ -time

6) Field _____ -tending

7) Street _____ Hog

8) Hack-A- _____ Fu

9) Ray _____ Iverson

10) Lay _____ and Down

11) New _____ Number

12) Half _____ -out

Bonus: ???

Only three NBA teams do not end with the letter S. Can you name all three?

Scrambled Schools

The names of some of the top NCAA schools, men's and women's, have been all mixed up.
See if you can unscramble them. Beware, this puzzle is tricky if you don't follow college ball.

1) Keud _____

2) Labroy _____

3) Tictocnecun _____

4) Calu _____

5) Axset _____

6) Anollvvia _____

7) Dorflia _____

8) Sipmhem _____

9) Manradly _____

10) Sul _____

11) Yukkcten _____

12) Onhrt Roilnaca _____ _____

In 2006-07, 350 NBA players came from Div. I schools, three came from Div. II, one from Div. III and 35 came straight from high school, while 53 players did not attend school in the USA.

Round and Round Again

Fill the answers to the clues into the grid below, beginning with #1 in the upper left corner, and working clockwise around the grid. The last one or two letters from each answer form the beginning of the next answer. If you can't get one clue, try moving on to the next and working backwards. The number in parentheses beside each clue indicates the number of letters in the answer.

1) _____ - Oop (5)

2) New _____ (4)

3) Romantic shot that goes in off the glass (4)

4) " _____ Man Award" (5)

5) One of the quarters (5)

6) All players do this (7)

7) King James' first name (6)

8) Shaquille, Jermaine (5)

9) Only city with two NBA teams (10)

10) Type of forward (5)

11) The 1995-96 Bulls only _____ ten times all season (4)

12) Kind of ball "The Professor", "AO" and "Hot Sauce" play (6)

13) Type of foul (9)

14) Franchise with most NBA Final appearances (6)

Bonus: ???

On November 29, 2000, Pope John Paul II was named the seventh honorary Harlem Globetrotter in front of 50,000 people at St. Peter's Square in Vatican City. How many of the other seven (an eighth was named in 2001) honorary members can you name?

1				2		3	
			9				
8				13			
							4
	12	14					
7	11				10		5
				6			

Bonus: ???

From 1990 through 2006, six different teams won the NBA
Finals. Can you name all six? Extra credit for the number of
Championships each team won in that time.

More Choice

See if you can pick the right answer.

1) What strange thing happened to the NCAA in 1967?

A) Slam dunks were made illegal.

B) Seniors were not allowed to compete in the NCAA Tournament.

C) The Division I Championship game was won by UCLA. The strange thing was, only 51 total points were scored. (UCLA beat Dayton 30-21.)

D) Due to a money-laundering lawsuit filed against the NCAA, there were no championships that year, in any division.

2) What is Dikembe Mutombo's full name?

A) Luba Dikembe Dikembe Mutombo

B) Dikembe Mutombo Mpolondo Mukamba Jean Jacques Wamutombo

C) Dikembe Fresh Mutombo

D) William Willford Wanahana Dikembe Wanzah Mutombo-la

3) What was the highest jersey number worn in the NBA in the 2006-07 season?

A) 55

B) 50

C) 93

D) 70

4) What does FIBA (the organization responsible for the World Basketball Championship and Olympic tournaments) stand for?

A) Fédération Internationale de Basketball

B) Formal Institution of Basketball Associations

C) Fun International Basketball Association

D) Fredrick Illsmere Basketball Union

5) Which one of the following has Ron Artest NOT done?

A) Been benched for two games for asking to have a month off (in mid-season) to promote his upcoming rap album.

B) Before his rookie season, he applied to work at electronics store Circuit City. Why? Because he wanted the employee discount.

C) Broke two of Michael Jordan's ribs in a pick-up game in June 2001.

D) Stopped at mid-court with the ball in a 2002 game against the Milwaukee Bucks to start "popping and locking," a hip-hop dance move.

Andrea Bargnani, Toronto's first pick in the 2006 draft, is the first European player to be drafted first overall.

What Am I? #2

See if you can figure out what these clues point towards, in as few clues as possible.

A

1) I'm usually sighted between May and August, though sometimes I show up in September.

2) I celebrated my 10th birthday in 2006.

3) One quarter of me is the 23rd letter.

4) Does this phrase ring a bell? "Silver Stars Shock and Sting Comets near the Sun in the Sky."

   What am I? _____

B

1) My name was originally a French circus acrobat's yell.

2) I require exactly two people.

3) I'm one of the most exciting things that happens on the court … well, not exactly on the court.

4) I start with a dish, and usually end with a slam.

   What am I? _____

Bonus: ???
Who were the top five highest-paid players in the 2006-07 season?

The Buzzer Beater

The player names below are listed according to their length. Fit them into their proper place in the grid; there is only one correct place for each word. To start, find the only eight-letter space for "Gelabale", and go from there. Good luck!

4 Letters
Ager
Bass
Diop
Hart

5 Letters
Bowen
Brand
Davis
Evans
Novak
Owens

6 Letters
Arroyo
Kapono
Oberto
Ruffin
Taylor

7 Letters
Blalock
Collins
Fortson
Korolev
Nachbar
Salmons
Skinner
Webster

8 Letters
Gelabale

9 Letters
Augustine
Jefferson
Spanoulis

Basketball is one of the only sports that can be traced back to an exact origin. It was invented by Canadian Dr. James Naismith in 1891 at a YMCA training school in Massachusetts. He invented the game during the winter, as a fun activity to keep the men in shape throughout the year.

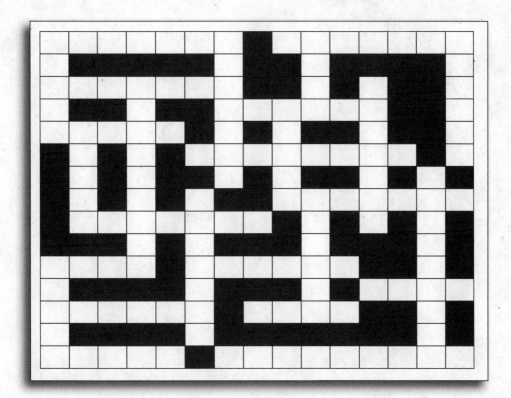

Top school? In 2004, the University of Connecticut became the first school to win both the men's and women's NCAA Division I tournaments in the same year. The women's team has won the title in 1995, 2000, 2002, 2003 and 2004 (going undefeated in '95 and '04). In 2006, Connecticut became the first school to have five players selected in the NBA Draft.

Globetrotters

Match these basketball stars with their native country.

Peja Stojakovic	Spain
Dirk Nowitzki	Canada
Yao Ming	Germany
Pau Gasol	Argentina
Manu Ginobli	Serbia and Montenegro
Tim Duncan	China
Dwyane Wade	Brazil
Tony Parker	France
Darius Songaila	U.S. Virgin Islands
Jamaal Magloire	Georgia
Zaza Pachulia	Slovenia
Nenê	USA
Rasho Nesterovic	Lithuania

For sixteen straight years, from 1965-1981, the MVP award was only won by a centre. Of course, it didn't help that Kareem Abdul-Jabbar and Wilt Chamberlain were both centres.

Quotables

See if you can figure out fact from fiction. Two of the player quotes are made up, but one is real. Circle the true quote. Yes, sometimes truth is stranger than fiction.

1) Shaquille O'Neal, on when he'll be able to return from an injury:

A) "What do I look like, a fortune teller? I ain't got no magic ball, man."
B) "I don't really care, I get paid either way."
C) "You put the toast in the toaster, and it ain't done until the toaster says, 'Ding.'"

2) Tony Kukoc, upon retiring:

A) "I announced my retirement yesterday, and this reporter asks me; 'Tony, didn't you retire last year?' I guess that's a good sign that it's time to go."
B) "I wish I could play until I was 100, but no one in the league will sign me to a contract! I should just start my own team."
C) "I always felt like I needed to play basketball. Right now, it's not my most desirable thing anymore. I'd rather play golf."

3) Charles Barkley, in a TV commercial selling his new brand of sneakers:

A) "These are my new shoes. They're good shoes. They won't make you rich like me, they won't make you rebound like me, they definitely won't make you handsome like me. They'll only make you have shoes like me. That's it."
B) "C-Bark here, sellin' some sneakers / Check the bass line, it'll blow ya speakers / My shoes will get you to the top / You can play like Sir Charles, make every shot / The Round Mound of Rebound raps with a better sound / The court is my hometown!"
C) "Hello fellow basketball fans, I'm Charles Barkley, and I have a royal guarantee: if you buy my shoes, I guarantee your game will improve! If you're not juking and jiving, driving and shooting like a pro with your new Barkleys, you get your full money back!"

4) Antoine Walker, on why he shoots so many threes:

A) "Because I'm good at it."
B) "Because there's no fours."
C) "Because I can't run very fast, so driving the lane isn't really much of an option."

Adrian Williams, selected 21st overall by the Phoenix Mercury, does more than just play. She is also an accomplished singer, and has performed the anthem at multiple Mercury games.

5) Kobe Bryant, on being thrown out of a playoff game:

A) "He didn't like my toneage, if that's a word. He's the decider. Is that a word, 'decider'?"

B) "The league likes to hand out big fines for talking bad about the refs, so I'm going to just donate $25,000 to charity instead, and say that was a great job by the striped shirts."

C) "I haven't been tossed from a playoff game in my career, so tack that on to my list of accomplishments."

6) Shaquille O'Neal, on Boston … we think:

A) "They shot the ball well early. What comes out of the microwave hot doesn't always stay hot. I know because I eat bagels in the morning."

B) "The Celtics are Irish. I like river dancing, but it's the kind of dance that you wouldn't want to know how to do, you know?"

C) "It was a fun game tonight. We won by 21 points. This afternoon I was playing NBA Live and lost to the Celtics by 5, so it was good to get some redemption."

7) Raptor Matt Bonner, when asked if there was resentment towards former teammate Vince Carter:

A) "Yes."

B) "Uh, yeah. I mean, it's tough to say, woulda, shoulda, coulda, ifs and buts like candy and nuts, you know, you never know. This, that, and the other thing. Who knows? You know, there's a lot of what-ifs."

C) "I wish I was a star player, and you reporters asked other players questions about me."

8) Mike James, after shooting only five of 25 field goals:

A) "It was a pretty good night, you know, if you were a tadpole or maybe an antelope or something. Antelopes got it real easy."

B) "Sometimes me and the rim just don't agree … I think I'm going to give her flowers and candy before the next game."

C) "The worst part is my whole family was in the crowd tonight; parents, brothers, cousins … they're going to give it to me later. They make fun of me anyway because my initials are MJ, but it's going to be even worse tonight."

A true athlete: Charlie Ward won the prestigious Heisman Trophy in 1993 for the best college footballer. That same year, he was drafted by the Milwaukee Brewers of MLB, and again in 1994 by the New York Yankees. He turned down both sports in favour of the NBA. He was selected in the first round of the '94 draft by the Knicks and began a successful 12-year career.

Call the Wilt

By changing only one letter at a time, can you make the top word become the bottom word?
Be careful, each letter you substitute as you go must make a new word.
See page 23 for an example.

1) Kidd

_____

_____

Miss

2) Call

_____

_____

Wilt

3) Team

_____

_____

_____

Ball

4) Ball

_____

_____

_____

Wade

5) Bird

_____

_____

_____

Came

6) Kobe

_____

_____

_____

Rims

Bonus: ？？？

Fourteen teams played in the WNBA in 2006-07.
How many can you name?

A Little More History

Circle which year these clues point towards.

- The Charlotte Hornets joined the NBA, making it a 30-team league.
- Despite having a team of stars, the L.A. Lakers were upset in the NBA Finals by the Detroit Pistons. In a battle of two newcomers to the WNBA Finals, the Seattle Storm took the title 2-1 over Connecticut.
- Dwight Howard, Emeka Okafor and Ben Gordon were drafted first, second and third overall.

2002   2003   2004

- The Women's National Basketball Association played its first season, with the Houston Comets winning the title thanks to MVP Cynthia Cooper.
- Tim Duncan, Keith Van Horn and Chauncey Billups were drafted first, second and third in the draft, while Tracy McGrady was not drafted until the ninth selection.
- Allen Iverson picked up the Rookie of the Year award, Karl Malone was the MVP, Miami's Pat Riley won Coach of the Year, and Dikembe Mutombo won his second of four Defensive Player of the Year awards.

1997   1998   1999

- At the 19th Summer Olympics, Yugoslavia won gold in the men's final, while the USSR took gold in the women's event.
- Larry Bird won Rookie of the Year honours, while another rookie, Magic Johnson, stepped up in the NBA Finals to lead the Lakers to the Championship, earning Johnson the Finals MVP award.
- The Dallas Mavericks joined the league, making it 23 teams. For the first time, the NBA finished a full season with the three-point line, permanently changing the game.

1968   1976   1980

Best number ever? Larry Bird, Kareem Abdul-Jabbar, Grant Hill, Scottie Pippen, Alonzo Mourning, Antonio Davis, Stephon Marbury and Patrick Ewing all wore #33 at one point.

Hidden Teams #3

Six NBA team names are hidden below, starting with the central letter M and extending out. The letters can be connected on either side, above, below or diagonally. The same letter cannot be used twice in the same name. We've used either the city or franchise name of the team (i.e., Houston or Rockets). Watch out, one name is hidden twice!

C	I	R	A	S	V	O	R	A
K	E	U	L	W	S	A	T	I
S	K	V	A	I	I	E	M	A
E	K	N	E	M	I	N	A	C
E	N	M	I	E	A	N	I	B
A	T	E	S	T	M	G	H	M
N	I	G	O	H	A	P	S	I

Bonus: ??!

Of the original 11 NBA teams from 1946, how many are still playing today in the same city? Can you name them?

Lost Letters #2

Fill in the missing letter in the middle to complete the last letter of the player's name on the left, and the first letter of the player on the right. The missing letters, taken from top to bottom, spell out the name of the oldest player to ever play in an NBA game (at 43).

Chris Webbe	_____	aja Bell
Rafael Arauj	_____	rien Greene
Cheick Sam	_____	rian Cook
Corey Maggett	_____	ddie House
Marshall Webste	_____	icky Davis
David Wes	_____	ayshaun Prince
DeSagana Dio	_____	aul Pierce
Yakhouba Diawar	_____	llen Iverson
Danny Grange	_____	ashard Lewis
Manu Ginobil	_____	ke Diogu
Baron Davi	_____	amuel Dalembert
J.R. Smit	_____	akim Warrick

* Oldest Player :

_____

Chick Hearn, the Lakers' legendary play-by-play announcer, broadcast a record 3,338 consecutive games from 1964 through 2001. He coined terms like slam dunk, air ball, finger roll and triple-double.

The World B. Free Puzzle

There have been some weird and funny names in the NBA. Can you spot the four made-up names from the list below?

Bonus: ❓❓❓

One of these players only played college ball. Can you spot him, too?

Pops Mensah-Bonsu	Thelton A. Baller
World B. Free	Uwe Blab
Honest Willtruth	Chief Kickingstallionsims
Rajon Rondo	God Shammgod
Hedo Turkoglu	Nenê
Krytnc Sykrndr	Kevin Pittsnogle
John Block	Bo Outlaw
Tree Rollins	Martynas Andriuskevicius
Boniface Ndong	Mo Momoson
Mamadou N'diaye	Zarko Cabarkapa

Alex Stivrins had a strange career. He played three games for Seattle in 1985-86, then not again until 1992-93 when he played 10 games for Phoenix. He was then traded to the Clippers (he played one game), Milwaukee (three games), and finally to Atlanta (five games). He retired after the season, having played 22 games in two seasons with five different teams.

Game Day

Fill in the crossword grid by answering each clue, corresponding to the number in the grid.

Across

1) Point/Shooting

4) Precedes "dunk"

6) Elite _____

7) Hoop

9) Lane

10) Home state of San Antonio, Dallas

11) Dr. J's last name (Julius _____)

14) "Pass to me! I'm _____!"

16) One way to create a turnover

18) Low - _____ Shot

Down

1) Someone who plays on the Harlem entertainment team

2) Common crowd chant

3) The 2006-07 Trail Blazers have the lowest average ____ in the league, at 24.8

4) Nash, Francis, Kerr

5) Type of defense (3 words)

8) Number of teams in the NBA playoffs

9) The only NBA franchise name that is actually a short-form

12) If a team gets hot, they often go on one of these

13) Type of clock, but not the shot

15) The "P" in RPG

17) Assists per game, abbreviated

The 2006-07 season began on Halloween ... spooky stuff for Carmelo Anthony, who got ejected from his season opener.

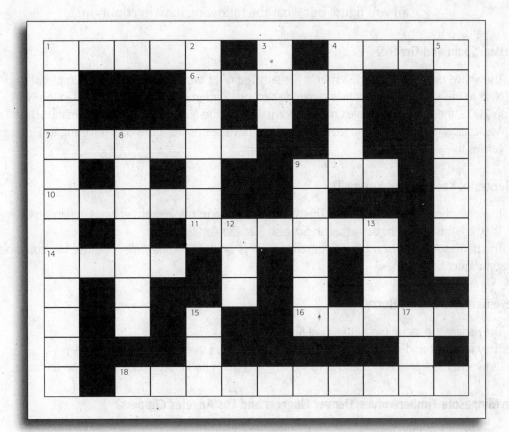

Bonus: ???

As of 2006, the Naismith Memorial Basketball Hall
of Fame has inducted 258 individuals (129 players,
70 coaches, 50 contributors and 12 referees) and
five full teams. Can you name the five teams?

What Do They Have in Common?

Can you figure out what the following have in common?

1) Russia, Spain and Greece?

A) They have eliminated the USA men's "Dream Team" at the last three World Championships.
B) Next to the USA, these countries have the second, third and fourth most players in the NBA.
C) In 2005, these three countries made a formal bid to the NBA to create the International Basketball Association (IBA). The proposed league would have teams from the USA travelling to Europe to play games there.

2) Baloncesto, Kosarka and Korvpall?

A) Together, they formed the "Triple Threat," a term given to the key players on Lithuania's Olympic team.
B) They are the words for basketball in Spanish, Croatian and Estonian.
C) The names Allan Iverson used to describe players on the Chicago Bulls, because he "could never remember their names."

3) Steve Kerr and Robert Horry?

A) They share the same nickname, "Big Shot Bob."
B) They rank first and second on the all-time list of playoff three-pointers.
C) Between 1994 and 2003, every NBA Champion team had either Kerr or Horry on its roster.

4) The Minnesota Timberwolves, Denver Nuggets and Los Angeles Clippers?

A) Through 2007, they have never reached the NBA Finals.
B) They were the only franchises that did not sell out at least one game in the 2006-07 season.
C) They are all owned by billionaire Glen Taylor.
D) All of the above.

5) The United States men's and women's national basketball teams?

A) In the 2006 World Championships, they both lost in the semi-final match and had to settle for bronze.
B) They are both ranked #1 in the world.
C) The only Olympics that both teams did not get a medal at was in 1980, when the USA did not participate.
D) All of the above.

The 2006-07 San Antonio Spurs have an average age of 30.37, almost four years above the league average and nearly seven years older than the Portland Trail Blazers.

6) Shaquille O'Neal, Chris Webber and Allan Houston?

A) They all have a master's in business administration (MBA).
B) They were the three highest-paid players in 2005-06, with a combined salary of $58,250,000.
C) They all have their own clothing line, sold by Adidas.

7) Ann Meyers and Lucy Harris?

A) They were the first female NBA players. Harris was drafted by the New Orleans Jazz, and Meyers signed a one-year contract with the Indiana Pacers. Neither ever played an NBA game.
B) Incredibly, they are the WNBA's co-leaders in career rebounds, both with 921. They both retired in 2006.
C) They helped create the WNBA. In 1995 they presented a bid to the NBA, and thanks partly to fan interest in women's basketball at the '96 Olympics, the league began play in 1997.

8) Aaron, Jason and Marvin?

A) For nine straight games in 2002, the New Jersey Nets only used players with those three first names.
B) They all share the most common last name in the NBA.
C) They are Dwyane Wade's middle names (Dwyane Aaron Jason Marvin Wade).

9) Karl Malone, John Stockton and Moses Malone?

A) They all share the same birthday, March 26th.
B) They all played their last NBA game at age 40, against the Charlotte Hornets.
C) They rank first, second and third on the all-time turnover list.

10) Natalie Williams, Cheryl Ford and Tamika Catchings?

A) They are first, second and third on the all-time WNBA steals list.
B) They all had fathers who played in the NBA (Nate Williams, Karl Malone and Harvey Catchings).
C) They were the top three scorers in the 2004 Olympics, all averaging over 30 points per game.

Bonus: ???

The majority of NBA players come from Division I colleges. Which schools sent the most players into the NBA in 2006-07? Can you name the top five?

College Stars

The names of 19 of the top-scoring collegiate players from recent years are hidden below. Only their last names are hidden, and the names are written forwards or backwards, hidden horizontally, vertically and diagonally. The leftover letters spell out the two teams involved in the biggest blowout in Division I history, 141-50.

T	R	N	O	S	N	H	O	J	U
Y	E	U	E	A	L	M	O	N	D
E	Y	F	S	S	L	S	S	A	D
K	A	A	A	H	B	N	N	B	O
C	F	D	T	Z	I	I	N	U	U
U	B	I	E	L	E	O	T	R	B
T	M	P	L	L	S	K	C	T	Y
S	O	O	S	I	E	L	A	T	R
A	C	I	R	R	A	K	I	S	E
V	L	R	I	R	N	E	E	R	G
B	O	O	K	E	R	I	A	L	B
M	H	E	K	C	I	D	E	R	W

Names

Kenny ADELEKE
Larry BLAIR
Steve BURTT
Andre COLLINS
Quincy DOUBY
Caleb GREEN
Trey JOHNSON

Elton NESBITT
Brion RUSH
Rodney STUCKEY
Morris ALMOND
Roy BOOKER
Keydren CLARK
Alan DANIELS

Nick FAZEKAS
Whit HOLCOMB-FAYE
Adam MORRISON
J.J. REDICK
Tim SMITH

The largest crowd to ever watch a basketball game was 78,129 at the BasketBowl, a game between Michigan State University and the University of Kentucky in late 2003. The previous record-holder was a 1951 Harlem Globetrotter's game at the Olympic Stadium in Berlin (75,000 fans).

Biggest Div. I Blowout:

___ ___ ___ ___ (141) VS. ___ ___ ___ ___ ___ ___ ___ (50)

Know More Teams

Can you figure out which NBA teams these clues point towards?

1) The only team that is also a fast food meal.

_____

2) This team breaks the sound barrier.

_____

3) This team is usually found on cowboy boots.

_____

4) This team helps make your engine go.

_____

5) This team goes places others have never been.

_____

6) The only team that is physically part of the basketball court.

_____

7) This team wears a royal crown.

_____

8) This team is a member of the feline family.

_____

9) A hairdresser might use this team.

_____

Bonus: ???

Can you name the top five all-time NBA leaders in total steals?

Word Work – Milwaukee

See how many words you can make using only the letters in "Milwaukee". They must be three letters or longer. We spotted 40; how many can you find? Here's the key:

0-10 words: High school player   30-35 words: NBA All-Star

10-20 words: College player   35-40 words: Hall of Famer

20-30 words: NBA substitute

MILWAUKEE

_____ _____ _____
_____ _____ _____
_____ _____ _____
_____ _____ _____
_____ _____ _____
_____ _____ _____
_____ _____ _____
_____ _____ _____
_____ _____ _____
_____ _____ _____
_____ _____ _____
_____ _____ _____
_____ _____ _____
_____ _____ _____

In 2006, Michael Jordan was the sixth-highest paid athlete in the world, pulling in $33 million dollars. The retired star still makes more than Kobe Bryant, who comes in eighth with $28.8 million. Tiger Woods tops the list, with a ridiculous $87 million.

Mixed Up Names

Amare Stoudemire
Brad Miller
Marcus Camby
Zydrunas Ilgauskas
Katie Douglas
Tamika Catchings
Lisa Leslie
Lauren Jackson
Sheryl Swoopes
Shawn Marion
Elton Brand
Andrei Kirilenko
Carmelo Anthony
Gilbert Arenas
Chris Paul
Kevin Garnett

The Great Search

** Leftover letters spell out Clyde "The Glide" Drexler.

In the Lane

1)	**O**	–	Yao Ming	7)	**O** –	Personal Foul
2)	**N**	–	Dunk	8)	**S** –	Basket
3)	**J**	–	Jordan	9)	**C** –	Celtics
4)	**V**	–	Travelling	10)	**T** –	Raptors
5)	**B**	–	NBA Finals	11)	**C** –	Cavaliers
6)	**O**	–	Triple Double	12)	**N** –	Rebound

** **Bonus:** Charlotte Bobcats, 2004. Vancouver (Memphis) Grizzlies, 1995. Toronto Raptors, 1995. Orlando Magic, 1989. Minnesota Timberwolves, 1989.

True or False

1)	True	9)	False
2)	True	10)	True
3)	False	11)	True
4)	True	12)	True
5)	True	13)	False
6)	False	14)	True
7)	True	15)	False
8)	False		

Dream Teams

Connecticut Ballers
Newark Statesmen
Trenton Marauders

Hidden Teams

Cavaliers
Celtics
Charlotte
Chicago
Cleveland
Clippers
* Chicago is hidden twice.
** **Bonus:** 2004 Men's: Argentina – Gold, Italy – Silver, USA – Bronze
2004 Women's: USA – Gold, Australia – Silver, Russia – Bronze
2000 Men's: USA – Gold, France – Silver, Lithuania – Bronze
2000 Women's: USA – Gold, Australia – Silver, Brazil – Bronze

Round and Round

1)	Charlotte	9)	Tie
2)	Team	10)	Eastern
3)	Minutes	11)	Nets
4)	Steal	12)	State
5)	All-Star	13)	Ten
6)	Rebound	14)	NBA
7)	Dallas	15)	Ballhog
8)	Shot	16)	GP

** **Bonus:** Nate Thurmond (1974 – 22 points, 14 rebounds, 13 assists, 12 blocks), Alvin Robertson (1986 – 12 points, 11 rebounds, 10 assists, 10 steals), Hakeem Olajuwon (1990 – 18 points, 16 rebounds, 11 blocks, 10 assists)
* **Note:** Blocks and steals have only been recorded since 1973, so it is likely Wilt Chamberlain, Jerry West and other stars of the day recorded the feat.

Lost Letters

Dwyane Wad	_E_	arl Watson
Jason Kid	_D_	amon Stoudamire
Joey Graha	_M_	alik Rose
Charlie Villanuev	_A_	mir Johnson
Nenad Krsti	_C_	hauncey Billups
Andre Iguodal	_A_	lan Anderson
Dan Dicka	_U_	ros Slokar
Charlie Bel	_L_	uther Head
Ronald Dupre	_E_	meka Okafor
Tracy McGrad	_Y_	ao Ming

* Missing letters spell out Ed Macauley, MVP of first All-Star Game
** Bonus: #2: LA Lakers, 14 titles #3: Chicago Bulls, 6 titles #4: Philadelphia 76ers, Golden State Warriors, San Antonio Spurs and Detroit Pistons, all tied with three titles (as of 2006)

Your Choice

1 – B	6 – A
2 – A	7 – B
3 – D	8 – C
4 – D	9 – A
5 – C	

Scrambled Terms

1) Backboard
2) Western Conference
3) Travelling
4) Buzzer Beater
5) Final Four
6) Fast Break
7) Defensive Rebound
8) Power Forward
9) March Madness
10) Free Throw
11) Technical Foul
12) Goaltending
13) Championship

** Bonus: Total Blocks: #1: Hakeem Olajuwon, 3,830 • #2 Dikembe Mutombo, 3,230 • #3 Kareem Abdul-Jabbar, 3,189 • #4 Mark Eaton, 3,064 • #5 David Robinson, 2,954

The Tip-Off

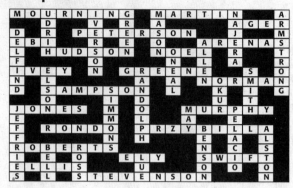

What Am I?

A – The Backboard   B – The Ball

Know Your Teams

1) Philadelphia 76ers
2) Chicago Bulls
3) Orlando Magic
4) Phoenix Suns
5) Utah Jazz
6) Toronto Raptors
7) Atlanta Hawks
8) Washington Wizards
9) Houston Rockets

** Bonus: The New York Nets (later moved to New Jersey), Denver Nuggets, Indiana Pacers and San Antonio Spurs

Skip to My Who?

Magic	-	Earvin Johnson
Air	-	Michael Jordan
The Answer	-	Allen Iverson
The Franchise	-	Steve Francis
Disco	-	Dirk Nowitzki
The Brazilian Blur	-	Leandro Barbosa
Dr. J	-	Julius Erving
The Mailman	-	Karl Malone
The Great Wall of China	-	Yao Ming
Skip To My Lou	-	Rafer Alston
The Big Dipper	-	Wilt Chamberlain
The Worm	-	Dennis Rodman
The Dream	-	Hakeem Olajuwon
Kid Canada	-	Steve Nash
Flash	-	Dwyane Wade

A Little History

1 – 2000   2 – 2003   3 – 1996

Word Work – Portland

Ado	Old	Rapt
And	Oat	Rat
Ant	Pad	Road
Aorta	Pan	Rod
Apt	Pant	Rot
Art	Par	Tan
Darn	Part	Tap
Dart	Pat	Tar
Dolt	Plan	Tarp
Dot	Plant	Tart
Drat	Plod	Toad
Drop	Plot	Told
Lad	Pod	Ton
Land	Port	Top
Lap	Portal	Trap
Lard	Pot	Trod
Load	Pro	
Lord	Prod	
Nap	Rad	
Nod	Pan	
Nor	Rant	
Not	Rap	

** **Bonus:** Andrea Bargnani (2006), Andrew Bogut (2005), Dwight Howard (2004), LeBron James (2003), Yao Ming (2002), Kwame Brown (2001), Kenyon Martin (2000), Elton Brand (1999), Michael Olowokandi (1998), Tim Duncan (1997)

It's a Numbers Game

1)	3,142		10)	14
2)	17,558		11)	57,446
3)	46		12)	38,378
4)	139,381,526		13)	6'7"
5)	41,333,581		14)	221
6)	136		15)	6'11"
7)	49		16)	5'9"
8)	82		17)	1
9)	30		18)	105,000,000

Pass the Buck

1) Mavs – Mass – Mash – Nash
2) Man – Tan – Tin – Tie
3) Rose – Pose – Post – Past – Pass
4) Pass – Bass – Bask – Back – Buck
5) Hook – Hoot – Soot – Shot
6) Dunk – Funk – Fund – Fond – Fold

* **Note:** There may be other ways to answer these correctly.

Opening Night

Across		Down	
1)	Captain	1)	Center
3)	Cap	2)	Travel
5)	March	3)	Camp
7)	Pass	4)	Personal
8)	Ewing	6)	Chicago
9)	Roll	10)	Olympic
12)	Fadeaway	11)	San
13)	Block	13)	Bump
17)	Miami	14)	Kidd
18)	Draft	15)	Goal
19)	End	16)	OT

Hidden Teams #2

Sacramento
San Antonio
Seattle
Spurs
Suns
SuperSonics

* Seattle is hidden twice.
** **Bonus:** Ranked eighth in 1985, Villanova is the lowest seed to win the NCAA title.

Dream Arenas

The Entertainment Palace
NEC/AMEX Center
The Rolling Stones Center

** **Bonus:** Total Assists: #1: John Stockton, 15,806 #2: Mark Jackson, 10,334 #3: Magic Johnson, 10,141 #4: Oscar Robertson, 9,887 #5: Isiah Thomas, 9,061

Still in the Lane

1)	R – Garnett		8)	A – NCAA
2)	T – Perimeter		9)	V – Mavericks
3)	D – Dribble		10)	S – Steal
4)	R – Warriors		11)	L – Ben Wallace
5)	M – Memphis		12)	P – Championship
6)	L – Clutch		13)	A – Team
7)	L – Carmelo Anthony			

Hard-Court Heroes

1 – D
2 – B – Only three times (32, 35 and 37 loss seasons) has a Jackson-coached team lost more than 27.
3 – D – Kobe has never won the MVP.
4 – C
5 – A
6 – B

Leading Ladies

** Leftover letters spell out (Taj) McWilliams-Franklin.

The Triple Dribble Puzzle

1) Orlando **Magic** Johnson
2) Jump **Shot** Clock
3) Triple **Double** Dribble
4) Sixth **Man** -to-Man
5) Turn **Over** -time
6) Field **Goal** -tending
7) Street **Ball** Hog
8) Hack-A- **Shaq** Fu
9) Ray **Allen** Iverson
10) Lay **Up** and Down
11) New **Jersey** Number
12) Half **Time** -out

** **Bonus:** The Orlando Magic, the Miami Heat and the Utah Jazz

Scrambled Schools

1) Duke
2) Baylor
3) Connecticut
4) ACLU
5) Texas
6) Villanova
7) Florida
8) Memphis
9) Maryland
10) LSU
11) Kentucky
12) North Carolina

Round and Round Again

1) Alley
2) York
3) Kiss
4) Sixth
5) Third
6) Dribble
7) LeBron
8) O'Neal
9) Los Angeles
10) Small
11) Lost
12) Street
13) Technical
14) Lakers

** **Bonus:** Honorary Globetrotters: Henry Kissinger (1976), Bob Hope (1977), Kareem Abdul-Jabbar (1989), Whoopi Goldberg (1989), Nelson Mandela (1996), Jackie Joyner-Kersee (1999), Reverend Jesse Jackson (2001)

** **Bonus:** NBA Champions: Miami Heat (2006), San Antonio Spurs (2005, 2003, 1999), Detroit Pistons (2004, 1990), LA Lakers (2002, 2001, 2000), Chicago Bulls (1998, 1997, 1996, 1993, 1992, 1991), Houston Rockets (1995, 1994)

More Choice

1 – A
2 – B
3 – C – Ron Artest wears #93.
4 – A
5 – D

What Am I? #2

A – The WNBA
B – Alley Oop

** **Bonus**: #1: Kevin Garnett, $21,000,000 #2: Chris Webber, $20,718,750 #3: Allan Houston, $20,718,750 #4: Michael Finley, $20,154,625 #5: Shaquille O'Neal, $20,000,000

The Buzzer Beater

B	L	A	L	O	C	K		N	A	C	H	B	A	R	
O				O			G							U	
W	E	B	S	T	E	R		E		C				F	
E		P		O	B	E	R	T	O				F		
N	O	V	A	K		O		V		O			I		
	W		N		G	E	L	A	B	A	L	E		N	
	E		O		V		A			I		J			
	N		U	F		S	K	I	N	N	E	R			
	S	A	L	M	O	N	S		A		S	F			
	I		R			S	P				F				
B	A	S	S		T	A	Y	L	O	R		E			
R				S			N		H	A	R	T			
A	R	R	O	Y	O		D	I	O	P		S			
N				N							O				
D	A	V	I	S		A	U	G	U	S	T	I	N	E	

Globetrotters

Peja Stojakovic	-	Serbia and Montenegro
Dirk Nowitzki	-	Germany
Yao Ming	-	China
Pau Gasol	-	Spain
Manu Ginobli	-	Argentina
Tim Duncan	-	U.S. Virgin Islands
Dwyane Wade	-	USA
Tony Parker	-	France
Darius Songaila	-	Lithuania
Jamaal Magloire	-	Canada
Zaza Pachulia	-	Georgia
Nenê	-	Brazil
Rasho Nesterovic	-	Slovenia

Quotables

1 – C	5 – A
2 – C	6 – A
3 – A	7 – B
4 – B	8 – B

Call the Wilt

1) Kidd – Kids – Kiss – Miss
2) Call – Wall – Will – Wilt
3) Team – Teal – Tell – Tall – Ball
4) Ball – Mall – Male – Made – Wade
5) Bird – Bard – Card – Care – Came
6) Kobe – Robe – Robs – Ribs – Rims

* Note: There may be other ways to answer these correctly.
** Bonus: Charlotte Sting, Chicago Sky, Connecticut Sun, Detroit Shock, Indiana Fever, New York Liberty, Washington Mystics, Houston Comets, LA Sparks, Minnesota Lynx, Phoenix Mercury, Sacramento Monarchs, San Antonio Silver Stars, Seattle Storm

A Little More History

1 – 2004
2 – 1997
3 – 1980

Hidden Teams #3

Magic
Mavericks
Memphis
Miami
Milwaukee
Minnesota

* Minnesota is hidden twice.
** Bonus: The New York Knicks and the Boston Celtics

Lost Letters #2

Chris Webbe	_R_	aja Bell
Rafael Arauj	_O_	rien Greene
Cheick Sam	_B_	rian Cook
Corey Maggett	_E_	ddie House
Marshall Webste	_R_	icky Davis
David Wes	_T_	ayshaun Prince
DeSagana Dio	_P_	aul Pierce
Yakhouba Diawar	_A_	llen Iverson
Danny Grange	_R_	ashard Lewis
Manu Ginobil	_I_	ke Diogu
Baron Davi	_S_	amuel Dalembert
J.R. Smit	_H_	akim Warrick

** Missing letters spell out Robert Parish, the NBA's oldest ever player, at age 43.

ANSWERS

The World B. Free Puzzle

Thelton A. Baller
Honest Willtruth
Krytnc Sykrndr
Mo Momoson

** Bonus: Chief Kickingstallionsims only played college ball.

Game Day

Across		Down	
1)	Guard	1)	Globetrotter
4)	Slam	2)	Defense
6)	Eight	3)	Age
7)	Basket	4)	Steve
9)	Key	5)	Man-to-Man
10)	Texas	8)	Sixteen
11)	Erving	9)	Knicks
14)	Open	12)	Run
16)	Steal	13)	Game
18)	Percentage	15)	Per
		17)	APG

** Bonus: The Original Celtics (an unstoppable team during the '20s, playing between 150-200 games a year in various leagues), The First Team (played with James Naismith in 1891), the Buffalo Germans (formed in 1895, won 111 straight games), the New York Rens (an all-black team that broke racial barriers in the '20s and '30s, eventually compiling a 2,588-539 record), The Harlem Globetrotters (travelling entertainment team, founded in 1926 and inducted into the Hall in 2002).

What Do They Have in Common?

1 – A
2 – B
3 – C
4 – A
5 – D
6 – B (Though Allan Houston retired on Oct. 17, 2005, he was still paid a full $19,125,000 salary.)
7 – A
8 – B (Their last name is Williams: 12 players in 06-07 shared that name.)
9 – C
10 – B

** Bonus: #1: Connecticut, 14 players #2: Duke, 13 players
#3: North Carolina, 12 players #4: Arizona and UCLA, 10 players each

College Stars

** Leftover letters spell out "Tulsa (VS) Prairie View".

Know More Teams

1) Denver Nuggets
2) Seattle SuperSonics
3) San Antonio Spurs
4) Detroit Pistons
5) Portland Trail Blazers
6) New Jersey Nets
7) Sacramento Kings
8) Charlotte Bobcats
9) Los Angeles Clippers

** Bonus: Total Steals: #1: John Stockton, 3,265 #2: Michael Jordan, 2,514 #3: Gary Payton, 2,443 #4: Maurice Cheeks, 2,310 #5: Scottie Pippen, 2,307

Word Work – Milwaukee

Ail	Lake	Maw
Aim	Lame	Meal
Ale	Law	Meek
Auk	Leak	Mew
Awe	Lee	Mewl
Awl	Leek	Mile
Eel	Lie	Milk
Eke	Like	Mule
Email	Lime	Wail
Ewe	Mail	Wake
Ilk	Make	Walk
Kale	Male	Weak
Keel	Maul	Wee
		Week